WARRIORS

KNIGHT

DEBORAH MURRELL

QEB Publishing

Published in the United States by
QEB Publishing, Inc.
3 Wrigley, Suite A
Irvine, CA 92618

www.qeb-publishing.com

Library of Congress Cataloging-in-Publication Data

Murrell, Deborah Jane, 1963-
  Knight / by Deborah Murrell.
     p. cm. -- (QEB warriors)
  Includes index.
  ISBN 978-1-59566-735-9 (hardcover)
  1. Knights and knighthood--Juvenile literature. 2. Civilization, Medieval--Juvenile literature. I. Title.
  CR4513.M874 2010
  940.1--dc22

                    2009003544

Author Deborah Murrell
Consultant Philip Steele
Project Editor Eve Marleau
Designer and Picture Researcher
        Andrew McGovern
Illustrator Peter Dennis

Publisher Steve Evans
Creative Director Zeta Davies
Managing Editor Amanda Askew

Printed and bound in China

Picture credits
Key: t=top, b=bottom, r=right, l=left, c=center
Alamy 10t INTERFOTO/History, 10c INTERFOTO/History, 11b The Print Collector, 15c North Wind Picture Archives, 17t Mary Evans Picture Library, 18l Paul Felix Photography, 21b jaxpix, 28l North Wind Picture Archives, 29l The Print Collector
Bridgeman Art Library 5r Bibliotheque Nationale, Paris, France, 18–19 Peter Jackson, 21t Musee des Beaux-Arts, Lyon, France, 26b Bibliotheque Nationale, Paris, France, 27t Angus McBride
DK Images 12r Geoff Dann
Getty Images 11t Edward Gooch/Stringer
Photolibrary 14b The Print Collector

Scala Archives 7t Photo Scala, Florence, 13c Photo Scala Florence/HIP, 20b Photo Scala Florence/HIP, 24b Photo Scala Florence/HIP, 25c Photo Ann Ronan/HIP/Scala, Florence, 29r Photo Scala, Florence/BPK, Bildagentur fuer Kunst, Kultur und Geschichte, Berlin
Shutterstock 10b EchoArt, 11c Anthro, 13b Johannes Wiebel, 32t Anthro, 32b Johannes Wiebel
Topfoto 9t Stapleton Historical Collection/HIP/TopFoto, 9b Columbia Pictures, 13t Topham Picturepoint, 13l AAAC/ TopFoto, 28b Topfoto/HIP

The words in **bold** are explained in the glossary on page 30.

Contents

What was a knight?

Knights were nobles who fought on horseback in the Middle Ages (AD 500–1500). They were the most powerful and feared fighters of their time.

FIGHTING FAMILIES

The kings, or other knights decided who could become a knight. If a man's father had been a knight, then it was likely he would be, too. Knights fought when their king or lord needed them in a battle. It was expensive to keep a horse. Armor and weapons cost a lot, too, so knights needed to be wealthy.

➤ *Knights were the most powerful fighting force on the battlefield and were feared by those on foot.*

CODE OF HONOR

Knights were so powerful that kings sometimes found them difficult to control. Some knights followed the code of **chivalry.** This was a set of rules for good conduct, or behavior.

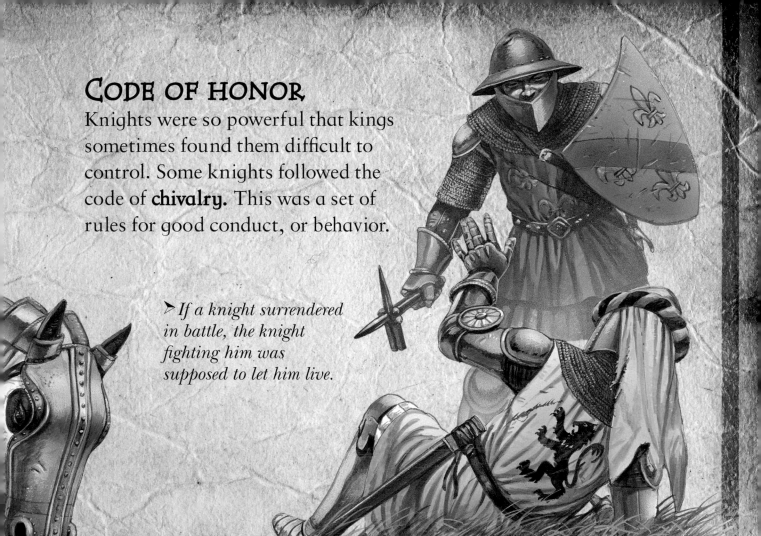

➤ *If a knight surrendered in battle, the knight fighting him was supposed to let him live.*

The Knights of the Round Table

Storytellers in the Middle Ages told exciting tales about a legendary king called Arthur and his chivalrous knights. They were said to have sat at a round table, so that none of them seemed more important than any of the others.

When did knights live?

Knights lived in Europe in the Middle Ages. Kings and nobles fought constantly for land and power. Knights defended their lord or king and fought in wars and battles at home and in other countries.

HOLY WAR

Jerusalem, in Israel, was a holy place for Muslims, Christians, and Jews. When Muslim Turks took control of Jerusalem in 1095, the Pope called for European Christians to lead a war of **religion**, or **crusade**, against them.

WARRIOR WISDOM

Most countries in Europe had a **feudal system**. The king owned the land, but lent it to barons and earls. They then gave land to lesser nobles and provided men as soldiers. The land was worked on by **peasants**.

SCOTLAND

IRELAND

North Sea

ENGLAND

WALES

ATLANTIC OCEAN

AGINCOURT ▲

Normandy

FRANCE

NAVARRE

LEON-CASTILE

ARAGON

CATALONIA

ALMORAVID EMPIRE

▲ *Knights fought against each other throughout Europe as well as in the Middle East.*

NORWAY

SWEDEN

DENMARK

Baltic Sea

POMERANIA

POLAND

HOLY
ROMAN
EMPIRE

HUNGARY

PAPAL
STATES

●Rome

BYZANTINE
EMPIRE

NORMAN ITALY

Antioch ●

Rhodes ●

Mediterranean Sea

▲ *Peasants who were owned by the lord were called* **serfs**.

FARMING THE LAND

Most peasants had to work on the lord's land, but there was some land to be shared by villagers as well. Open land was plowed into long, narrow strips. Peasants had to work hard for very little reward.

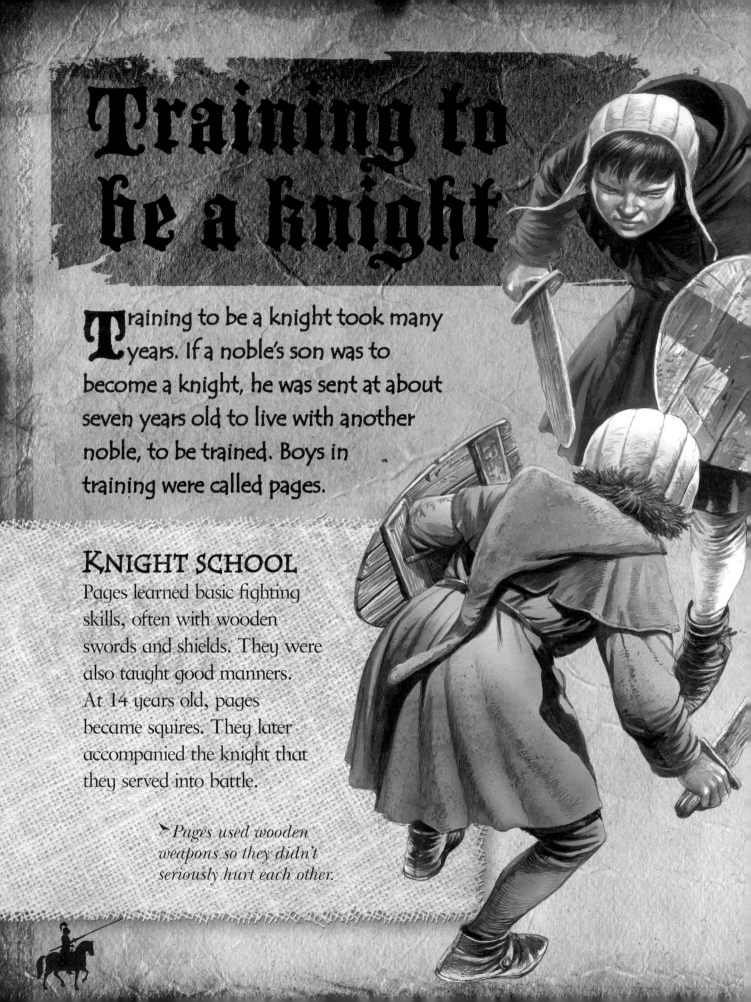

Training to be a knight

Training to be a knight took many years. If a noble's son was to become a knight, he was sent at about seven years old to live with another noble, to be trained. Boys in training were called pages.

KNIGHT SCHOOL

Pages learned basic fighting skills, often with wooden swords and shields. They were also taught good manners. At 14 years old, pages became squires. They later accompanied the knight that they served into battle.

➤ *Pages used wooden weapons so they didn't seriously hurt each other.*

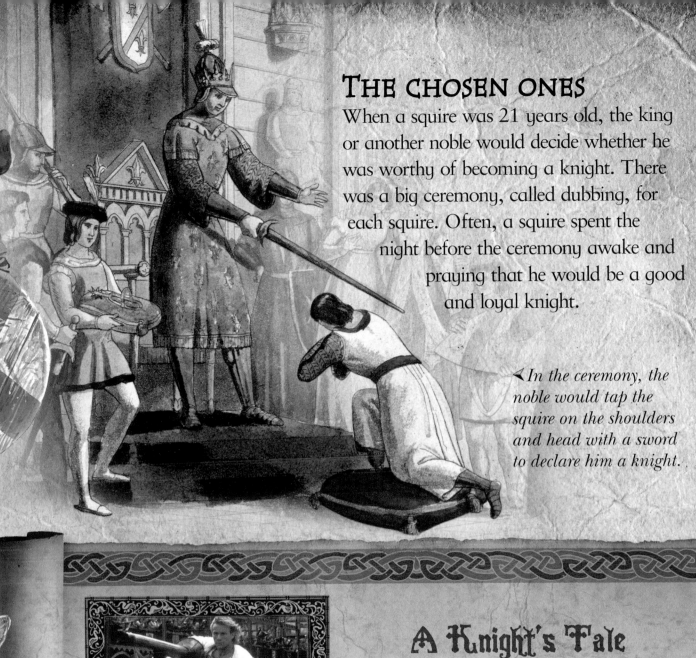

THE CHOSEN ONES

When a squire was 21 years old, the king or another noble would decide whether he was worthy of becoming a knight. There was a big ceremony, called dubbing, for each squire. Often, a squire spent the night before the ceremony awake and praying that he would be a good and loyal knight.

◄ *In the ceremony, the noble would tap the squire on the shoulders and head with a sword to declare him a knight.*

A Knight's Tale

The 2001 film A Knight's Tale, starring Heath Ledger, told the story of a young squire who entered **jousting tournaments** *after the knight he worked for died. He used a different name so he could pretend to be a knight.*

Weapons

Knights needed different weapons, depending on whether they were on the ground or on horseback, charging forward. Each weapon had its own uses at different stages of a battle.

Heavy metal head

MACE

A mace had a metal or wooden handle and a metal head. A good blow from a mace could knock a knight off his horse.

POLEAX

A poleax was often used by foot soldiers. The ax blade could slice through flesh and even armor.

Blade

SWORD

A sword was a metal weapon with a sharp blade. It had a crossguard to stop the holder's hands slipping down the blade.

Crossguard

Godfrey de Bouillon

Godfrey de Bouillon led the First Crusade in 1096. This was a battle for an area called the Holy Land in the Middle East. People said he was so strong that he once beheaded a camel with his sword.

Handle

DAGGER

A dagger was used for stabbing the enemy at close range. In the middle of a battle on the ground, a dagger could be more useful than a sword.

Sharp edge

LANCE

A lance was a long, wooden weapon with a sharp metal point. It was usually carried by knights on horseback. They held out their lances in front of them when they charged at the enemy.

Knights used lances to knock each other off their horses.

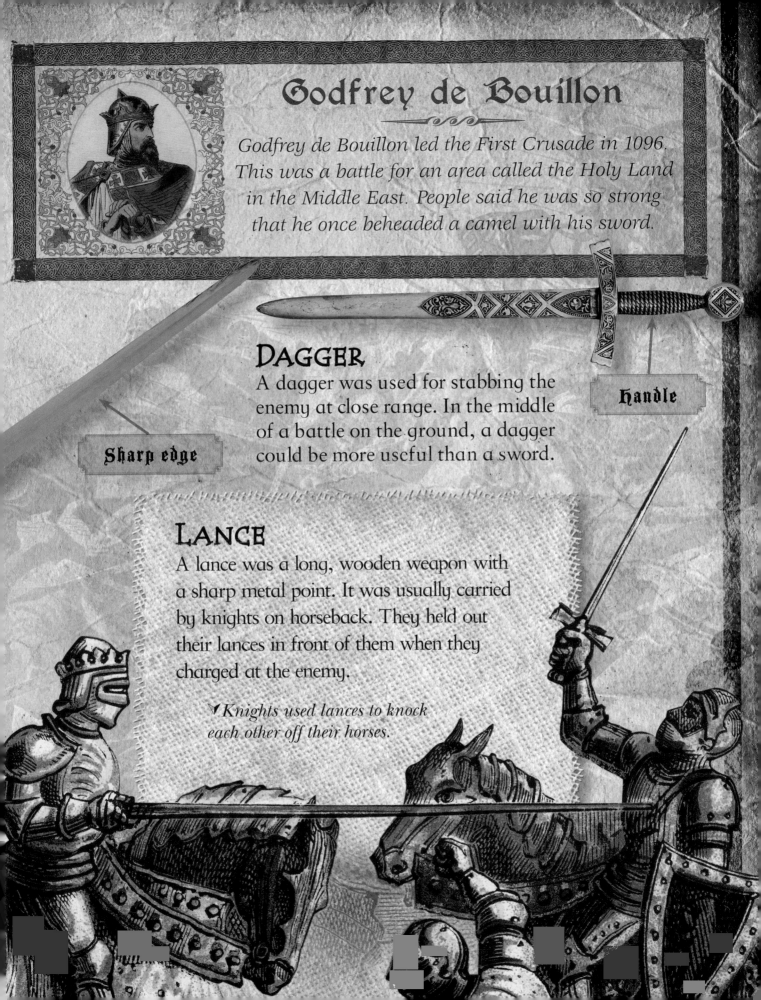

Armor

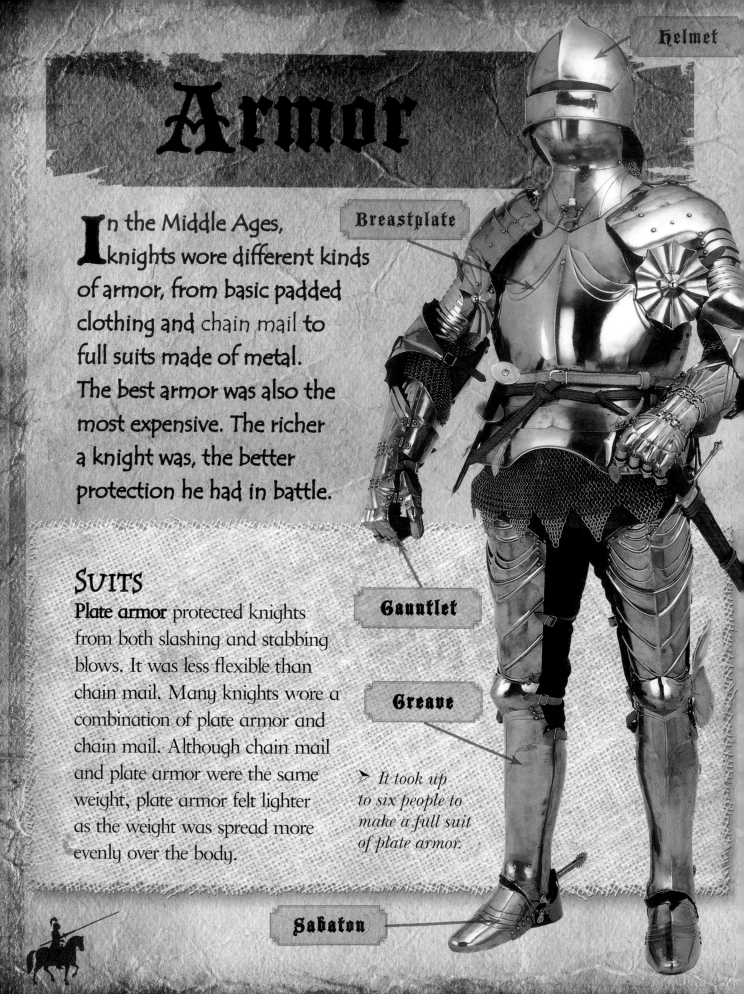

Helmet

Breastplate

In the Middle Ages, knights wore different kinds of armor, from basic padded clothing and chain mail to full suits made of metal. The best armor was also the most expensive. The richer a knight was, the better protection he had in battle.

SUITS

Plate armor protected knights from both slashing and stabbing blows. It was less flexible than chain mail. Many knights wore a combination of plate armor and chain mail. Although chain mail and plate armor were the same weight, plate armor felt lighter as the weight was spread more evenly over the body.

Gauntlet

Greave

➤ *It took up to six people to make a full suit of plate armor.*

Sabaton

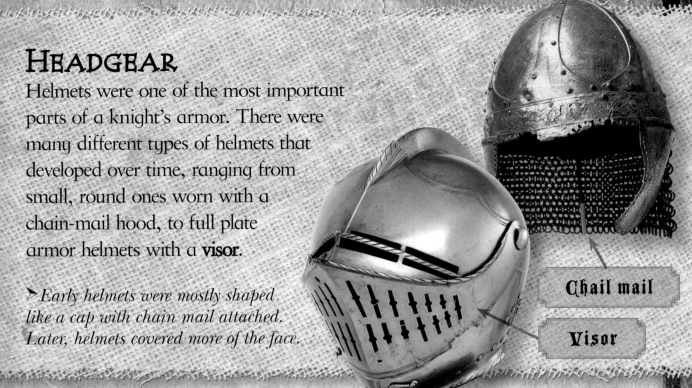

HEADGEAR

Helmets were one of the most important parts of a knight's armor. There were many different types of helmets that developed over time, ranging from small, round ones worn with a chain-mail hood, to full plate armor helmets with a **visor**.

➢ *Early helmets were mostly shaped like a cap with chain mail attached. Later, helmets covered more of the face.*

Chain mail

Visor

LINKING RINGS

Chain mail was made of lots of tiny metal rings linked together. It was very flexible, and it protected the wearer from being slashed by a sword. However, the rings could be forced apart by a stabbing blow. Chain mail rusted easily and was difficult to clean.

◄ *Chain mail could be made into a hood, tunic, or even pants.*

SHIELDS

A knight used his shield to protect his legs as well as his body. He carried his shield on the opposite side to his fighting arm.

➢ *The lion on the shield is "rampant" (on its back legs).*

horses

Rich knights often had more than one horse. Many had one for traveling on, and another for carrying their belongings. Heavier, stronger horses were used on the battlefield. A knight's horses were probably his most valued possessions.

> *A horse had to be strong to carry the weight of its own armor, as well as a knight's.*

HORSE ARMOR

A horse's armor was very important. The richer the knight was, the better his horse's protection would be. The most basic armor was a piece of padded cloth called a caparison, which covered the horse's whole body. Some horses even wore plate armor.

*Caparisons sometimes had a symbol, or **coat-of-arms**, to help identify the knight.*

Saddle

The high back of a saddle was called a cantel. The pommel, or high front, protected the knight's stomach and stopped him from being thrown over his horse's head.

Shaffron

The shaffron protected the front of the horse's head and ears. Some shaffrons had raised areas around the eyeholes so that the horse could not see straight ahead. This stopped the horse being startled, or scared, in battle.

Peytral

The most important part of the horse to protect was the chest. Chest armor was called a peytral. Not all knights could afford armor for their horses as well as themselves. If a knight's horse was hurt, it would put him in danger in battle so, if he could afford to protect his horse, he would.

Stirrup

The knight placed his feet in stirrups. This helped the knight to stay in the saddle when he was hit by another knight's lance.

Horseshoe

If a horse has to walk on wet ground for a long time, its hooves become soft and its feet sore. The knight's horse had a piece of metal called a horseshoe nailed onto each hoof to protect it. Horseshoes are still used today.

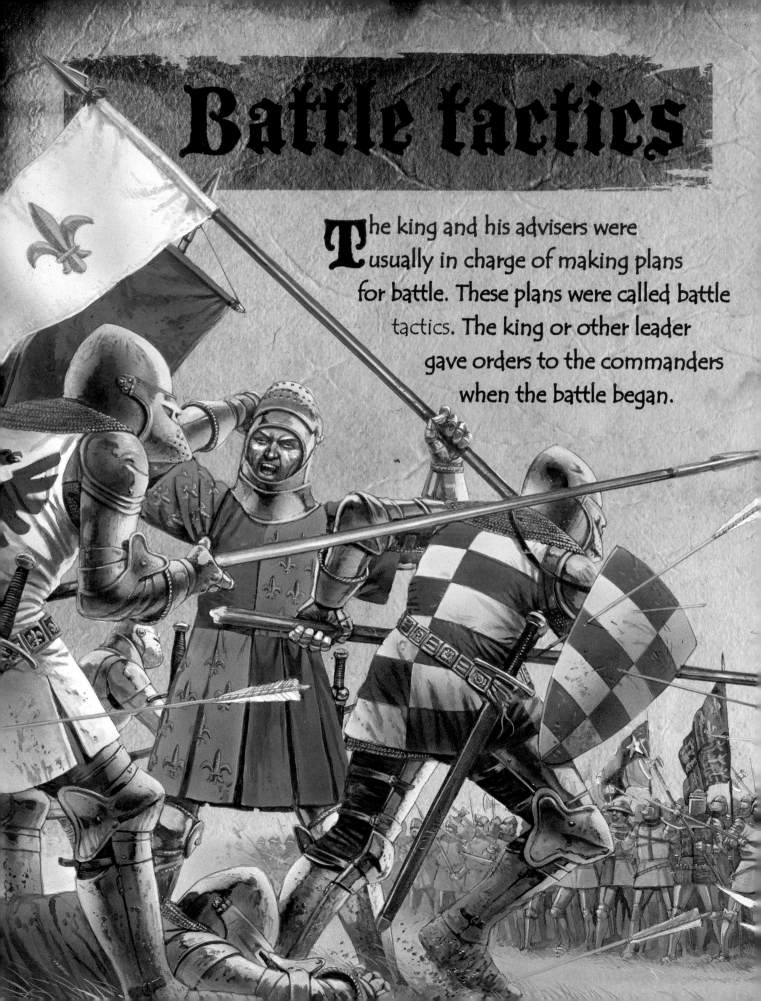

Battle tactics

The king and his advisers were usually in charge of making plans for battle. These plans were called battle tactics. The king or other leader gave orders to the commanders when the battle began.

Richard the Lionheart

King Richard I of England (1157–1199) was given the nickname "Lionheart" because of his bravery in battle. At 16 years old, he led his army to victory against his father's enemies in France.

IN COMMAND

Before the battle started, the king told the commanders what the tactics were. Once fighting began, it was not easy to change the plan. The commanders were far away from each other, so it was difficult to speak to all of them at once. Horns and flags signaled the start of the fight and showed **troops** where to go on the field.

▼ *The troops at the front of the French army, the vanguard, carried banners as they moved toward the English during the famous Battle of Agincourt (1415).*

BATTLE FORMATION

Commanders had to make plans about where the groups of soldiers and knights would be positioned within the whole army. This was called a battle formation. Some soldiers used weapons called pikes. These soldiers were often placed at the front of the army, to frighten the enemy **cavalry** unit's horses.

On the battlefield

The medieval battlefield was bloody and noisy, and it was often difficult to know who was an enemy and who a friend. Arrows whistled overhead, often killing soldiers before they even had a chance to fight.

◁ A good archer could fire more than ten arrows in one minute.

▽ The English longbowmen attacked the French knights as they approached.

HERE COMES THE CAVALRY

In battle, knights rode on horseback in groups called cavalry units. Sometimes they would use a tactic called a cavalry charge, when the knights would ride very fast toward the enemy. As the knights were high up on horses, they could attack enemy foot soldiers. Knights on horseback charging forward could be a terrifying sight.

THE BATTLE OF AGINCOURT

The Hundred Years War began in 1337 and ended in 1453. It was a war between the English and French over who should rule France. In 1415, the most famous battle in the Hundred Years War took place. This was the Battle of Agincourt. England's king, Henry V, led his soldiers to Agincourt, France. It had rained, and the battlefield was covered in mud. French soldiers became stuck in the mud, making it easier for the English army to attack. Many French soldiers were killed, but fewer English soldiers fell. Henry V won the battle.

Heralds and heraldry

Sometime around the 1100s, knights began putting symbols on their shields so they could be recognized. These were soon added to coats that knights wore over their armor. The symbols became known as a coat-of-arms. This system of symbols was called heraldry.

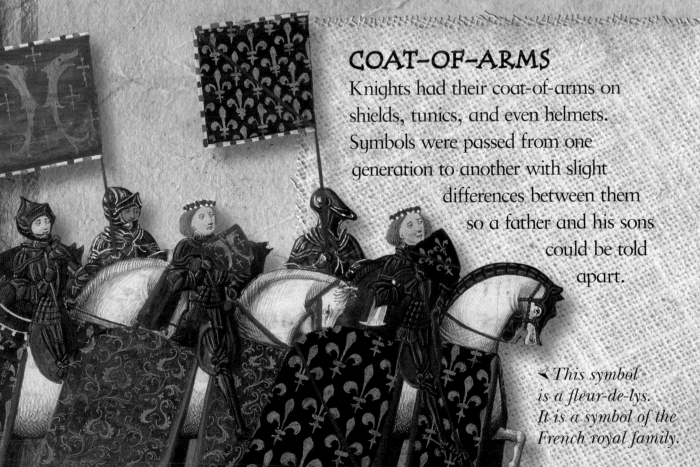

COAT-OF-ARMS

Knights had their coat-of-arms on shields, tunics, and even helmets. Symbols were passed from one generation to another with slight differences between them so a father and his sons could be told apart.

◄ *This symbol is a fleur-de-lys. It is a symbol of the French royal family.*

WHO WERE HERALDS?

In jousting tournaments, heralds were in charge of identifying and announcing the knights. Knights also took heralds to battle, where they carried messages from one commander to another. Heralds kept records of knights' coats-of-arms and created the system of heraldry.

➤ *In jousting tournaments heralds blew horns to signal the start of the competition.*

Order of the Garter

*The Order of the Garter is the most important honor a knight can be given in England. Today, there are fewer than 30 knights with this title. One of these knights is the Prince of Wales. The order's emblem is a garter with the **motto**, "shame upon him who thinks evil of this" in French. King Edward III started the Order in 1348.*

Castle under attack

Castles were the residences of important nobles and kings. They were large because they were built to protect the lord and his family, as well as the local villagers who worked on the land.

THE FIRST DEFENSES

Some castles were built on a hill. Often, a castle had a large **moat**, or ditch, built around it, to stop attackers from getting in. A **drawbridge** across a moat made it possible for people to enter a castle. This was lifted up if the castle was under attack.

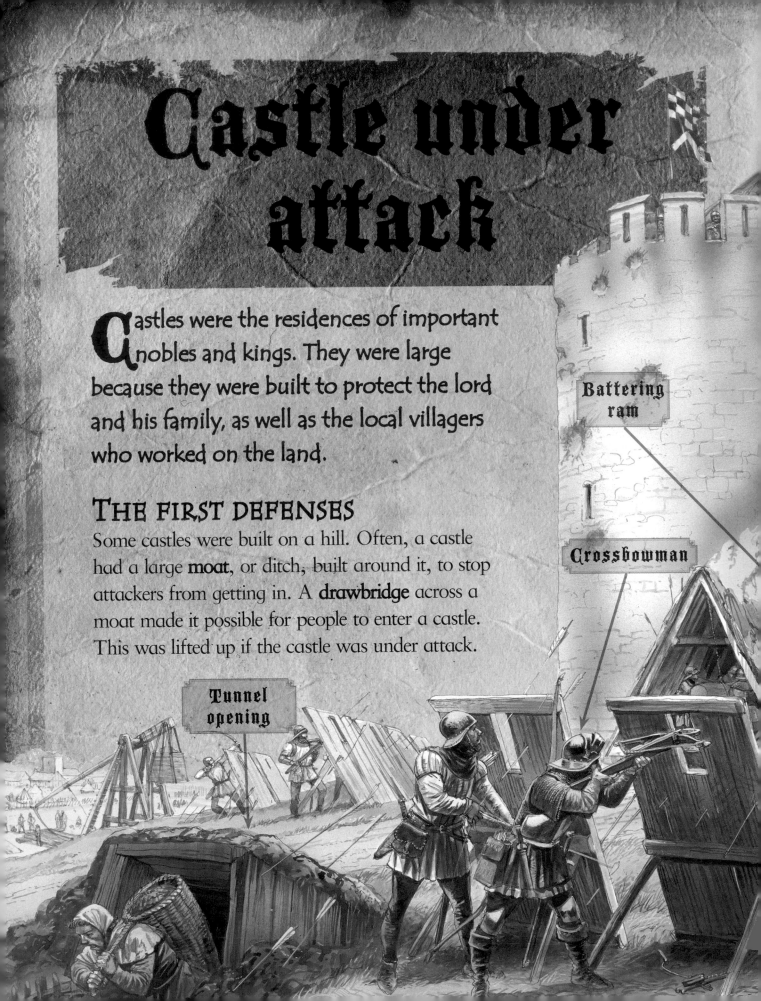

Battering ram

Crossbowman

Tunnel opening

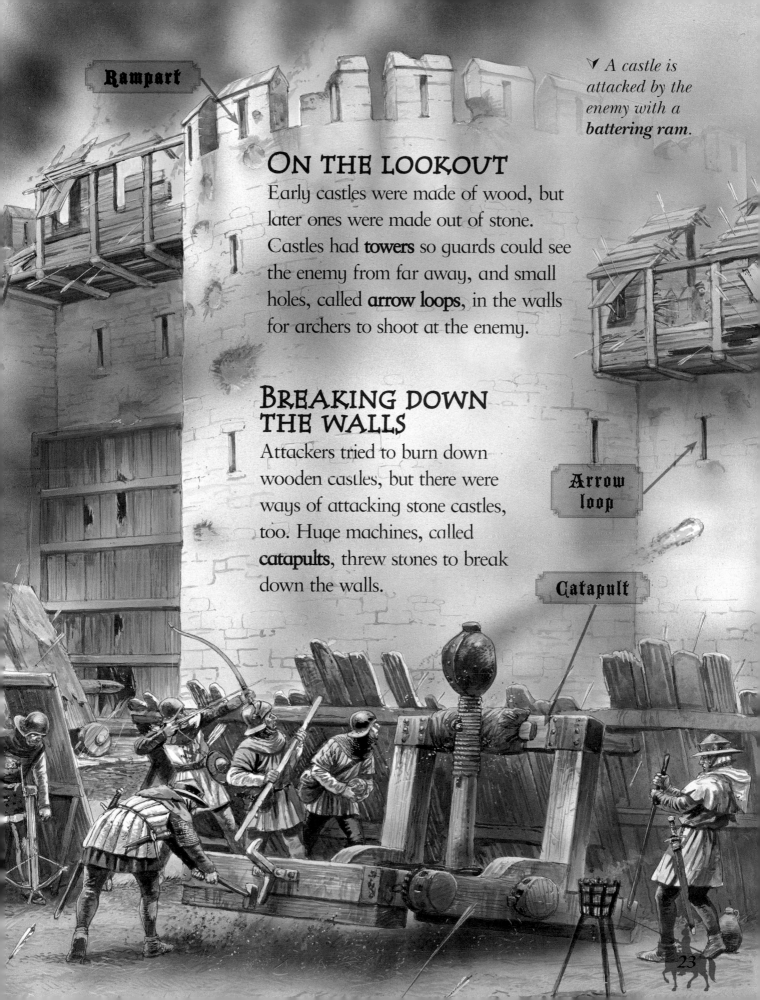

Rampart

▼ *A castle is attacked by the enemy with a* **battering ram**.

ON THE LOOKOUT

Early castles were made of wood, but later ones were made out of stone. Castles had **towers** so guards could see the enemy from far away, and small holes, called **arrow loops**, in the walls for archers to shoot at the enemy.

BREAKING DOWN THE WALLS

Attackers tried to burn down wooden castles, but there were ways of attacking stone castles, too. Huge machines, called **catapults**, threw stones to break down the walls.

Arrow loop

Catapult

Off the battlefield

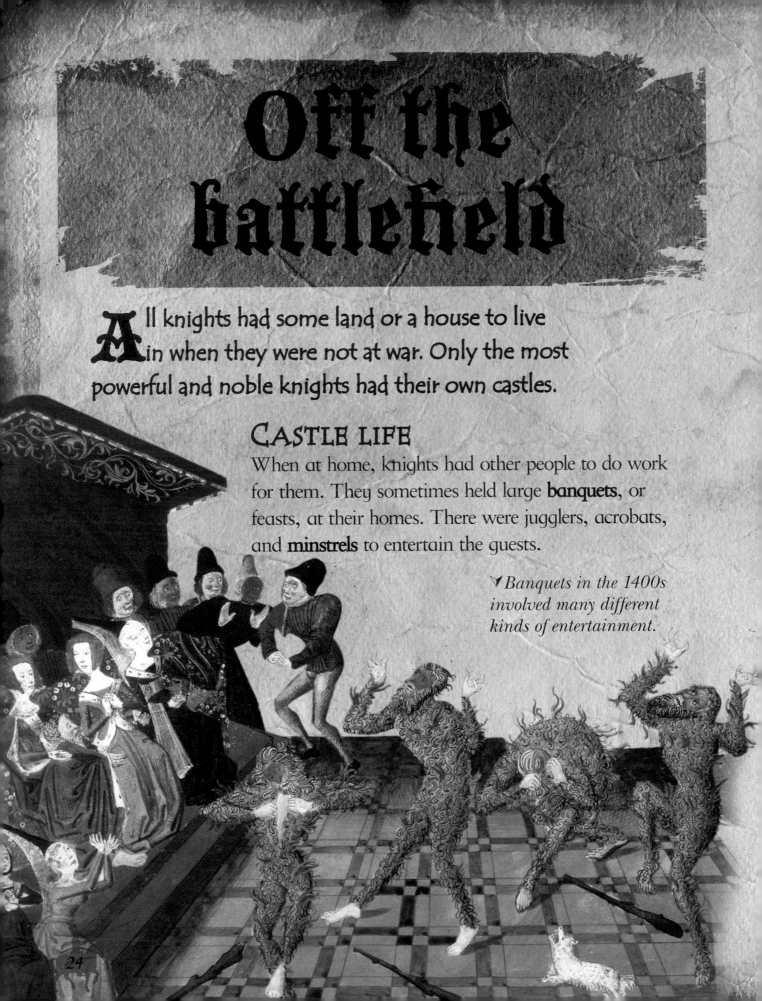

All knights had some land or a house to live in when they were not at war. Only the most powerful and noble knights had their own castles.

CASTLE LIFE

When at home, knights had other people to do work for them. They sometimes held large **banquets**, or feasts, at their homes. There were jugglers, acrobats, and **minstrels** to entertain the guests.

▾Banquets in the 1400s involved many different kinds of entertainment.

HUNTING AND HAWKING

Knights rode horses to hunt large animals, such as deer or boar, and used dogs to sniff out and chase the animals. Knights and ladies also enjoyed hawking, when they hunted small animals using birds. They caught a wild bird and trained it to kill small animals.

▶ Stag hunting was seen as a noble sport. Only the most powerful lords and ladies hunted stags.

WARRIOR WISDOM

In the Middle Ages, people mostly ate food that was grown or hunted on their land. They also shopped at markets for food that they could not get at home. Markets sold different kinds of food, such as fish.

Tournaments

When they were not at war, knights held tournaments, or fighting competitions. Tournaments helped knights to practice for battle. Soon, these tournaments became a popular form of entertainment.

PRETEND BATTLES

In each tournament, there were many different events. Mêlées, or pretend battles, were the earliest kind of fighting in a tournament. The knights were separated into two teams. Each team had to try to capture prisoners from the other, but there were very few rules.

▼ *King René of Anjou (1409–1480) enjoyed watching tournaments.*

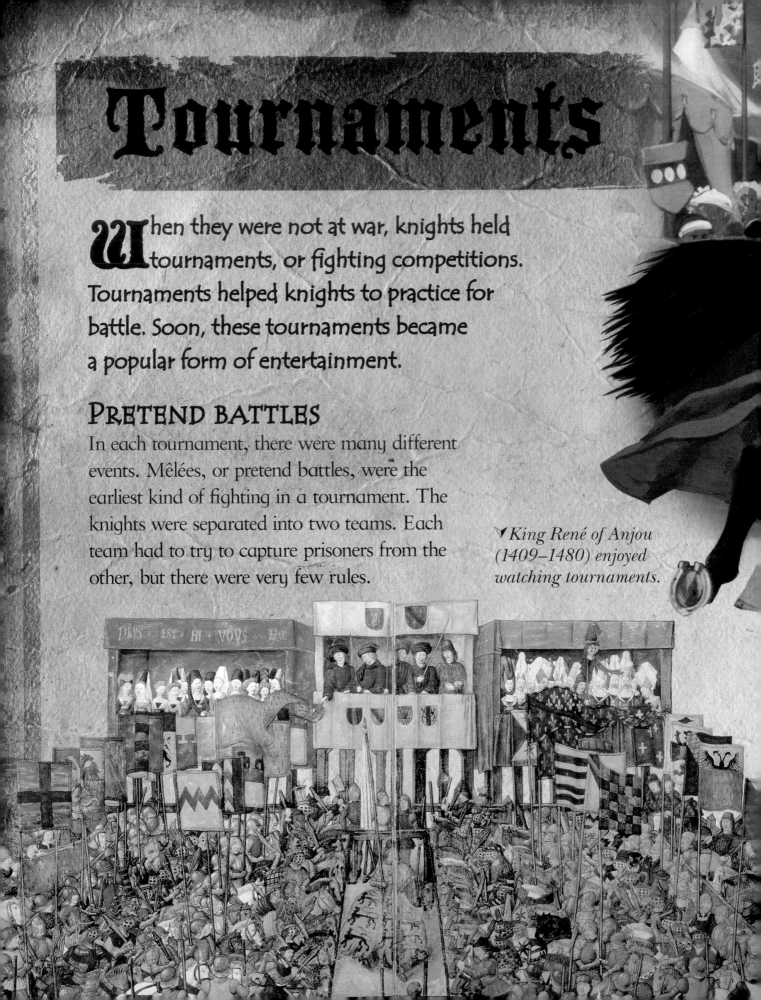

▲ *Knights used lances in jousting competitions as well as in battle.*

WARRIOR WISDOM

When Edward I of England fought Scotland and Wales in the 1200s, he had to ban jousting tournaments. Too many of his men were fighting in competitions instead of fighting in the real battles.

ONE-ON-ONE

Jousting was a battle between two knights. They rode toward each other and tried to knock one another off their horses. If one of the knights succeeded, he was awarded maximum points. Knights also scored points for good fighting skills.

The decline of knights

Toward the end of the Middle Ages, knights became less important in battles. Kings began to use paid soldiers, called mercenaries, to fight for them. These soldiers were always ready for battle.

NEW WEAPONS

In the late Middle Ages, longbows were powerful enough to shoot through plate armor. By the 1300s, cannon and guns had been developed, too. These new weapons became the strongest force on the battlefield.

◀ Guns were such powerful weapons that soon knights were no longer needed.

◀ Longbows were used to fire arrows at the enemy from a distance.

The Knights Templar

The Knights Templar were an order, or group, of knights that stayed in the Middle East after the First Crusade. They set up banks, built castles, and had a huge fleet of ships. In 1312, the Church said that some of the order's beliefs were un-Christian, and their order was banned.

TRADE

In the 1500s, new routes across land and sea were found. **Merchants** became wealthy by buying and selling goods such as spices and silk—sometimes they were wealthier than kings! Kings made many merchants into knights. By this time, the title of "knight" was just an honor, and had nothing to do with fighting.

◄ *Merchant ships traveled all over the world to trade goods.*

Glossary

Archer A soldier who fights with a bow and arrows.

Arrow loop A narrow slit in a castle wall where archers stood to fire arrows at attackers.

Banquet A feast, or meal, for many people.

Battering ram A large beam used to break down a wall, door, or gate of a building.

Catapult A machine used to throw large or heavy objects.

Cavalry Soldiers on horseback.

Chain mail A kind of armor made of tiny metal rings linked together.

Chivalry A code of good behavior that knights were supposed to follow.

Coat-of-arms A set of symbols that stands for a person, family, or country.

Crusade A war in which Christians fought for religious reasons.

Drawbridge A bridge over a moat that can be lifted up to stop attackers from getting inside a castle.

Feudal system A system that orders people depending on how important or powerful they are. A king would be at the top and a peasant would be at the bottom.

Gauntlet A kind of glove covered in metal.

Greave A kind of armor worn on the leg.

Heraldry The system of recording the symbols, or coat-of-arms, that knights had.

Jousting tournament A one-on-one competition in which one knight tried to knock the other off his horse.

Mercenary A soldier who is paid to fight for a foreign country or lord.

Merchant Someone who buys and sells goods such as silk, perfume, and fabric.

Middle Ages A period that lasted between about AD 500–1500 in Europe.

Minstrel A singer or musician.

Moat A ditch dug around a castle to help protect it from enemies.

Motto A phrase that describes the intention or beliefs of a group of people.

Noble Someone from a powerful or wealthy family. There were different kinds of nobles, such as lords, barons, and earls.

Peasant A poor person who worked on the land.

Plate armor A kind of armor made of plates of metal, shaped to fit around the body.

Rampart A stone wall that protects the castle.

Religion A form of worship that is practiced according to a kind of belief system.

Sabaton Part of a knight's armor that covers the foot.

Serf A peasant who had to work on a lord's land in return for protection.

Tactic A carefully planned action.

Tower A tall structure built to give a good view of the land around a castle.

Troops Soldiers in an army.

Visor Part of a helmet that can be pulled down to protect the face.

War A long period of fighting between different countries, states, or armies. Many battles may be fought in a war.

Index